ARRAS

MEMORY BEWITCHED

Photography **Jean-Pierre DUPLAN** and **Éric LE BRUN**
Text **Hervé LEROY**
Translation **Gillian KENNEDY** and **Cyrille DIVRY**

PASSAGES EN VILLE [ECO-VERSION]
LIGHT MOTIV PUBLICATIONS

PREFACE

If you ask somebody to write a preface for a book, you may well have assumed he or she likes the subject of the book. So as I have been asked to write the preface for this book on Arras, you may have assumed that I like Arras.

So I ask myself, do I like Arras ?

I would have a few good reasons for not liking Arras. I spent my childhood in its dampness and humidity with a sky the colour of a dirty dishcloth looming above my head and a vengeful God threatening me with Hell.

At an early age I was thrown out of St Joseph's Institute for putting the Virgin Mary down the toilet.

The bourgeois of Arras have not always been kind to me, son of a *father who never killed anyone.*

I bear no grudges, I love Arras.

Perhaps I love it because of all the mischief I got up to there.

Perhaps it's because I can still hear the echo of clogs ringing in the alleyways from the days when my brothers and I raced through them.

Perhaps it's because of the Scarpe, the river where, equipped with just a piece of string, you could catch sticklebacks.

Perhaps I love it because of the fortifications of Vauban where we used to play at soldiers.

Perhaps it's because of the great organ of the Church of Saint Nicolas en Cité which always gave me goose pimples.

Perhaps because of the imposing white cathedral where, for a while, I gave up Satan and his rituals.

Perhaps it's because of the smiles of the daughters of the bourgeois of Arras.

Perhaps because of the Casino where I saw Roberto Benzi, only 7 years old and still in shorts, conduct the Symphony Orchestra.

Perhaps because of the concert hall where I first heard Alfred Cortot play Chopin.

Perhaps because of the local theatre where I saw Jean Weber perform in 'L'Aiglon' by Rostand.

Perhaps because of the Festival d'Arras where, thanks to Reybaz, I discovered theatre.

Perhaps because of the Art Museum where I first began to appreciate painting.

Perhaps because of the public gardens where I discovered modern literature. Malraux's 'Condition Humaine' I read in the Minelle garden. In the 'Allées' garden I read 'l'étranger' by Camus; in the 'Saint Vaast' garden I read Sartre's 'Nausée'.

At Arras we don't die in ignorance..

I love Arras.

Maybe it's because of the slopes of Artois, where on my bike, I would fight the North wind.

I still can see the musical notes floating out of the belfry, the polystyrene notes that I had thrown from the top of the Belfry for a television film. Thanks to the North wind the notes circled around in the sky above, floated around the Belfry for a while as the bells played, before landing in the gardens among the astonished gardeners.

Maybe I love Arras because of the vastness of the sky as dawn breaks.

It maybe because of the Squares.

One day I wanted to film the Main Square, with a Paillard and Bolex 16mm camera, to illustrate Brel's song:

'Sur la place chauffée au soleil une fille s'est mise à danser...'

« In the sun-bathed square a girl started dancing... ».

I found the square but I couldn't find the girl. I wanted to pay tribute to Hitchcock with a short film entitled 'But who killed Arras ?' The murderer was called Sunday.

I think I must know Arras inside out. As a child, in pyjamas and a blanket across my shoulders, I spent whole nights in cellars with my family and neighbours from the street of la Paix, reciting the Rosary in order to not receive a bomb on our heads. Fifteen years later in the same cellars transformed into night clubs I was living it up...

When I look at the cover of this beautiful book, I feel I would like to end my days in one of the houses on the Main Square from which I would be able to watch Arras waking up. I could very well see myself at the window on the left...

next to the beautiful lady from Arras.

Jean-Louis Fournier, Film director, Writer

Most recent book : *Où on va papa* ? Published by Stock, Prix Fémina 2008

CONTENTS

TOWN SQUARES AND MURMURS

« Les beffrois ont été élevés pour que ceux qui grouillent à leurs pieds soient incités à lever les yeux et le front, à apprendre qu'il est une ouverture qui crève leur niveau à deux dimensions et s'échappe dans une troisième, découvrant et créant l'altitude. »

René Huyghe

A city risen like the Phoenix from its own ashes, rich in arches and spiral scrollwork, Arras is full of charm. Sited at the crossways where the lines of war and lines of influence intersect, with each rebirth the city's beauty is enhanced; it endures, a free and independent spirit.

Through the centuries, what common thread has been spun by man's ingenuity and his faith in the future?

History greets you at every street corner. The gentle Northern light doesn't abrade the local stone; it caresses it, and stimulates your palette of sentiment and emotion. The past has no separate existence; it is an accretion of the present, and of ever-expanding time.

Arras is two cities, or rather a heart with two ventricles. On one side the *Cité* and the episcopal powers. On the other side the town and its magistrates. To the West, the ancient *Nemetacum* which has become the district of the Prefecture. To the East the town dating from the Middle Ages which has developed around the *Abbaye Saint-Vaast.*

What is most surprising is the way the space constantly opens out and then closes in again. What other town in the world offers similar - contrasting - perceptions? Within just a fraction of a second an alley of just a metre wide opens into a square of seventeen thousand m^2 !

There are things that you show and things you keep to yourself. The magnificent *Place des Héros.* In the shady alley, *rue de la Batterie,* the merchants would once have dealt with their disputes.

Within and Without

Lines of convergence, cul-de-sacs, small oval or round squares, the octagonal *Place Victor Hugo,* the moon-shaped fish market, high walls and courtyards. Arras combines striking examples of the urban concept and community life on the one hand with the preservation of utmost privacy. A town with geraniums at the windows and cats at the curtains. As our eyes survey the immensity of *Grand'Place* they fall first on a grinning mask, next on the gentle softness of a stone face, then on a woman with the tail of a mermaid.

Each and every street and square is a new universe for the eyes.... and ears; from the loud cries of the market, the *Ducasses* (local fairs), the water jousting and other local festivals to the murmuring of secret conversations.

Rides and clearings within a forest of stone? Not only that: the town is full of surprises. Arras is a city in a country setting. Within its bounds, we can only guess at the existence of the four hectares of the walled *Jardins de la Prefecture;* and just outside,

◄ The 'Bastion des Chouettes' (Bastion of the Owls), with the Citadel; some of the last remains of the fortifications of Arras.

the Crinchon that the *Atrébate* clothes and fabrics were re-nowned. The *Rue aux Foulons* marks where the cloth was fulled; the *Place de l'Ancien Rivage* marks where the barges pulled alongside. From the *Jardin Minelle,* which is watered by the springs of the fish breeding grounds, we come back to the Méalens basin, then to the Scarpe and the *Écluse Saint-Nicolas.* At the foot of the falls, amongst the mallards and the cries of the gulls we can fish for roach, trout and pike.

One of the reasons that Vauban's project went ahead in 1668, at the expense of the neighbouring hills, was that the Crinchon could be used to flood the moat.

The citadel of Arras was part of the *Pré Carré,* a double line of fortified towns aimed at protecting the kingdom against invasion by the Spanish-controlled Low Countries. In fact, the beautiful but useless *"Belle Inutile"* was principally aimed at keeping an eye on the town. The King of France mistrusted his new subjects. Royal and Military power, Episcopal power, power of the Echevins; this town of the plains is multi-faceted even in its geography. The hills of Baudimont and of La Madeleine, the low lying quarters of the Méalens and the eighteenth century *basse ville* mean that the pedestrian is constantly going uphill or downhill. So, what mysterious alchemy has led to this mira-culous balance which has survived from the depths of time?

Between *Grand'Place, Rue de la Taillerie* and the *Place des Héros* stand one hundred and fifty five gable-ended houses linked by a covered portico composing an architechural feature unique to Europe. Arch after arch, punctuated on the ground by three hundred and forty five sandstone columns. Volute after volute, rolling the sky like a sheet, leaving the heart touched by an extraordinary sense of harmony and serenity. Here the soul of Arras is to be found, in the permanent balance between public and individual success.

the *Jardin Minelle* (Minelle Garden) is a romantic trysting-place for lovers.

On the inside, space closes in around the gardens of the *Abbaye Saint-Vaast;* On the outside it spreads luxuriantly over the *Square de la Légion d'Honneur.* The *hôtels particuliers* keep up appear-ances on the side of the entrance courtyard, saving the privacy for the gardens within.

On the walls ivy and wisteria play leapfrog with the white stone and red brick. Here and there a virginia creeper winds its way beneath a glass roof...On the outside, a green pathway between the *Jardin du Gouverneur* and the moat of the Citadel links the *cité* to the wheat fields.

The Memory of Water

The town was born at the confluence of the Crinchon and the Scarpe. The name Arras is possibly a contraction of *Atrébates* to *Ars,* which then became *Aras.* However, etymologists derive the word from the Celtic word *Ar,* which means 'running water'. Used for the dyeing of fabric, retting linen and washing the wool; it was to a large extent owing to the qualities of the the water of

The Méaulens wet docks and river quay.

◄ Contrary to what Verlaine sings, the poet is not always right; the lion which has its throne on the top of the Belfry is not the lion of Flanders... but the lion of Arras!

Verlaine speaks of the *"squares intoxicated with air and with the songs of the swallows"* At the *Place des Héros*, the poet sings the praises of the belfry of his home town...

*"Majestic, high above the land
stands for all time the mighty tower
of a gothic belfry, hanging in the sky
avowing the duties and the rights of the past.
And high above it the great lion of Flanders
roars with a voice of gold at the modern world:'Take it if you dare!'"*

Built between 1463 and 1554 the belfry is surmounted by the crown of Charles Quint and the Lion of Arras, a symbol from the coat of arms of Baudoin, Lord of the Manor at the end of the twelfth century. Radiating power, the lion holds a standard bearing the form of the sun...which was added at the time of the incorporation of Arras into France by Louis XIV. Seventy-five metres above ground symbols of history jostle at close quarters.
"The belfries were erected so that those swarming at their feet would be encouraged to lift their eyes and appreciate that they had the opportunity to break out of their two-dimensional outlook and escape into a third dimension and higher level of existence," records the writer and Arras-born academic René Huyghe. The stone, the squares, the spirals and monuments are not simply a stage setting, they have been moulded by human history, by the suffering, aspirations and dreams of the people of Arras. *"The immense Northern plain which appears to be level is in continuous dialogue with the sky. Where could a grander platform be found to erect a belfry which would confer nobility on its town – and its people?"*

An edict of Philippe II stipulates: *"No one shall have the right to build in the town of Arras unless the walls are built of stone or brick and do not overhang the streets"*. In spite of this no two houses are the same. Each one has its own dimensions and its own decorative style. The bell at the entrance of *Grand'Place* which chimes the opening of the grain market, cloth tied in bows, goblins, sheafs of corn, cherubs, cockerels, a snail in its shell, a mermaid, a salamander, a unicorn, a whale; page by page the squares reveal a fantastic series of images.

The Belfry and the Town Hall, lighting designed by Cabinet Bideau.

UPSIDE DOWN

« Les mots de la langue humaine ne peuvent suffire à qui se hasarde dans les abîmes du globe. »

Jules Verne

What lies beneath our feet? To what dark region of our mind does this subterranean world return us? We ascend to the seventh Heaven. We descend into Hell. Below the camping site on *Rue du Temple,* beyond the barrier of black shale at the entrance to the cavern – where do these hundred and ten steps lead? Towards which kingdom of Hades? Cerberus, Eurydice and Orpheus are all here on the staircase.

Twenty metres further down, a silence peopled with echoes, a constant temperature of eleven degrees and eighty percent humidity weighing on the shoulders. Thoughts turn to Jules Verne. *"Words of mortal language cannot be adequate for those who venture into the depths of the earth"* In this journey to the heart of Arras there is no never-ending ocean, no *"skies of vapours"*, no *"lizard-headed"*, *"porpoise- snouted"* or *"crocodile-toothed"* sea monsters!

Beneath the *Atrébate* ground, beneath the station, beneath the quarters of Ronville and Saint-Sauveur, the reality is more human, more moving. It looms up in the torchlight. There, in charcoal, the elegant form of a woman wearing a hat. Beautiful coal dark eyes against a background of chalk. Love rubs shoulders with death. PA Bowting from Bournemouth has engraved a crucifix into the wall *"in memory of the comrades killed in action on 14th April 1917."* Like a totem, the bust of Donald McKenzie, soldier of the 7th Canadian division 15th platoon, surges forward out of the stone. Human traces are all around; shrines, tributes to King George V of England, a Maori poem, benches to relax on, mess tins, three pronged forks, cans converted into candlesticks, secluded "sleeping galleries" for officers, latrines, transmission cables.

"Elsewhere can be found an actual field hospital of 700 places" says Alain Jacques, one of the town's archaeologists.

At the foot of pillar 5E emotion oozes from the pores of the cavern. Just ahead of the assured hell of the hail of bullets, what record has the chalk retained of this last mass on 8th April 1917. How many soldiers climbed to the front using this wooden ladder which led straight into the German trenches, this "exit 10"? How many never returned?

By the end of 1916 the town is on its knees, flattened, annihilated by the continued bombing. Above ground there remain a mere thousand or so die-hards. Below ground twenty four thousand men are preparing in the utmost secrecy. According to the plan drawn up by General Nivelle and General Haig, Arras is the rear base from which the British troops have to create a diversion ahead of the offensive along the fronts of Soissons and Reims. History comes to the rescue of the Allied forces – the subsoil of the town is like a Swiss cheese. Worked until the eighteenth century, the chalk quarries form veritable subterranean cathedrals. The tunnellers from the New Zealand Tunnelling Company open out the *Boves* – the legendary cellars of *Grand'Place* - bore tunnels through to the quarries to the Southeast of the town, and reach a point right under the noses and the beards of the German lines. A colossal achievement! A genuine Trojan Horse for troglodytes, shaking itself out over 22 kilometres of galleries and tunnels.

"It is the largest underground site of the First World War; six months of uninterrupted work, finishing only 6 days before the battle on 9th April 1917," enthuses Alain Jacques in admiration.

Many tons of spoil are stored in the unoccupied galleries. Secret chambers are crammed full of explosives in case the enemy should discover this amazing underground town. Mains water and electricity is also installed. Black shale is dumped at the entrance to mislead possible German spies and to avoid tell-tale traces of chalk above ground.

Underground, the tunnellers recreate the map of New Zealand. From North to South we go from Russell to Bluff, passing through Auckland, New Plymouth, Wellington, Nelson, Blenheim, Christchurch or Dunedin. In order to keep their bearings the British regiments do the same, naming the quarry where they are stationed – *"two hundred men to three hundred square metres"* – Glasgow, Carlisle, Liverpool, London or Manchester. The quarries that are furthest out are named after the islands; Jersey, Guernsey or Alderney. On 9th April 1917, at first light of dawn comes the great day. At 5.30am twenty thousand allied soldiers rise up out of the ground, emerging from the underground tunnels, through openings blasted out with explosives and rush towards the German trenches at Bois-les-Boeufs. The Germans are taken completely by surprise. At Tilloy a group of German officers have their breakfast abruptly terminated. Two whole enemy divisions are captured at Saint-Laurent-Blangy. The Anglo-Canadian soldiers take out the first lines, neutralising twenty thousand German soldiers and reaching Vimy Ridge.

Unfortunately the main offensive at *Chemin des Dames* is a failure. From 14th April the Germans receive significant reinforcements and the breach cannot be fully exploited. The breakthrough isn't decisive but the enemy front line is forced back by ten or so kilometres. The battle of Arras does succeed in freeing the town from the deluge of fire and remains as the only allied victory of 1917.

Underground, in the galleries rediscovered by Alain Jacques and his team in the 1990s, the record remains intact, as if the chalk had absorbed everything. Such an exceptional heritage could not be left in obscurity. There was a strong desire to provide some kind of special setting in memory of the sacrifice of the twenty four thousand English, Scottish and New Zealand soldiers. The Wellington Quarries, or Carrières Wellington, opened to the public on 1st March 2008. At the entrance a memory wall, a memorial in the form of a living museum, a journey below ground following a trail laid out over three hundred and fifty metres which enables us to appreciate the everyday life of the soldier. The faces, the eye-witness accounts are all there. The jokes in the face of death are still legible. We can hear the sound of the harmonica, killing time before the attack. It is only rust that has settled on the metal utensils ...and not only from the damp in the atmosphere. Emotion is very near the surface.

The 'Boves', the underground tunnels under the 'Place des Héros' (Heroes Square). ➤

Quelle nuit fantasmatique se cache derrière ces passages dérobés, ces vagues de voûtes, ces traces immémoriales ?

Underground Surprise

Storerooms for vegetables or barrels of beer and wine; warehouses for important market days; grain silos; foodstores for use in case of invasion; Second World War refuge; fallout shelter during the Cold War, Arras has always been at ease with its subterranean assets.

Between the Belfry where the lion keeps its throne and the *Boves*, twelve metres below ground, the centuries pile up on each other. Arras can be revealed vertically. Below the stylish surface, the shock of the underground. Below the gold of *Grand'Place* are other crow-stepped vaults, other cross-ribbed vaults, other spiral staircases: a negative of the town, riddled with caves and caverns.

The mining of the chalk dates back to ancient times. For over two thousand years man has been digging the ninety thousand year old rock beneath his feet. In Arras the ground has been dug in order for man to display his prosperity for all to see. It is with these blocks of chalk that Arras, the "white city", built its prestigious buildings and its town wall in the years following 1100.

What fantastic night is hiding in these concealed passages, these waves of vaults, these ancient remains?

The town's underground is its subconscious; place of dreams, inspiring myths and symbols.

Each year in Spring the visual artist Luc Brévart takes the galleries into the imaginary, scattering them with orchids, ferns, ivy and carnivorous plants and flowers. The *Boves* become an amazing garden. Lemon trees and fig trees bear fruit metres underground. It is pure pleasure and sheer madness. A memory re-invented.

With complete disregard for scientific reality, every self-respecting inhabitant of Arras will claim that the underground tunnels of *Grand'Place* go underneath both the Scarpe and the Crinchon, and lead to the ruins of the *Abbaye du Mont-Saint-Eloi.*

Doors, grills, bolts, labyrinths, stairwells, wan light which in turn darkens and becomes the depth of night and of time; the mystery remains. The mystery unfolds on a town with a hollow, an infinite space of uncertainty and darkness. Desire is stronger than the dark of night.

The 'jardin des Boves' (tunnel garden), designed by Luc Brévart. ➤

TRUTH AND LEGEND

La légende sert à justifier la présence de ces vestiges mégalithiques dont les hommes du Moyen Âge ne connaissaient plus l'origine...

Nightfall at the foot of Mont Saint Eloi is when the diabolical powers set about their work. The Merovingian Queen Brunehaut made a pact with the devil, agreeing to give him her soul on one condition; that he build a road between Arras and Théouanne before daybreak. Nothing was more simple than to light up the chicken run to get the cockerel to crow before sunrise. Humiliated and furious for having been fooled the devil threw two blocks of sandstone over his shoulder which became embedded upright in the Artois landscape. The stones of Acq are still scanning the skies. The larger of the two twin stones measures 3.3 metres and weighs eight tons.

The Legend attempts to explain the presence of these megalithic remains which man in the Middle Ages could not otherwise understand... Without doubt this Celtic sandstone from three to four thousand years BC was used for sun or burial rituals.

Brunehaut was unable to take her trickery with her to heaven; she died with her hair attached to a runaway horse on the straight stretches of the road that bears her name...in fact a roman road.

The Bear and the Saint

Arras is a land steeped in legends. Saint Vaast was however a real life character. He is thought to have been born in Villac in Perigord. What is more certain is that we later find him living as a hermit in Toul. We're in the era of the *Vase de Soissons*. In Tolbiac in 496, just when all seems to have been lost Clovis vows that he will convert to Catholicism if *"Jesus, who his wife claims is the son of the living God"* assures him victory against the Alamans. On Christmas day, the King of the Franks was baptised at Reims together with *"more than three thousand of his army"*. Vaast becomes his catechist; the legend is born...

Saint Vaast is despatched to the North of the kingdom where he heals the blind and the lame. Arras is in the hands of the "barbarians"and all that has been created to celebrate the glory of God is overgrown with brambles. The church has fallen to ruin and a bear has made its den within. Once the Saint starts to pray the bear, now gentle, comes out of its den, allows itself to be tamed and returns to the forest. Paganism is defeated.

The Saint dies on 6th February 540 as a *"nuée ardente"*(blazing cloud) is seen ascending into the sky. One final development takes place one morning in 668 in Baudimont from where the Bishop of Cambrai, Saint Aubert, sees a heavenly vision which invites him to lay the remains of Saint Vaast to rest in a church on the other side of the Crinchon. The Abbey is born. The town grows. Right up until the revolution a bear is said to be fed within the walls of the Abbey. The *Rue aux Ours* (Bear Street) remains as a reminder of this.

The minstrels and the candle

Like the squares at the heart of the town, the heroic deeds of history remain engraved in the hearts of the people of Arras.

April 2005: people hurry and jostle at the entrance of the *Musée des Beaux Arts* (Museum of Fine Arts) for the opening of an exhibition celebrating the nine hundredth anniversary of the miracle of the Sainte Chandelle. In this burst of popular fervour how can we separate the sacred from the secular and the tradition from the religion? Each year from Whitsun to Assumption the *neuvaine* or nine days of Notre-Dame-des-Ardents is one of the high points of life in Arras.

A priest of the parish sets the scene: *"An epidemic strikes as a punishment for the excesses and sins committed by the people of Arras. The air is so foul and corrupt that the inhabitants are taken with a strange sickness"*. The year is 1105. In fact the people of Arras are not at fault, the culprit is a fungus *'Cleviceps Purpurea'* – a mould – which causes small growths on cereal. Consumption of the rye ergot causes diarrhoea, vomiting, hallucinations, brain haemorrhage and gangrenes. In the face of such a terrible sickness confused words fill the air... *sickness of the fervent; sacred fire; the fire of Saint Antoine...*Science seems powerless, all that remains is faith.

During the night of 24th to 25th of May 1105 two minstrels, Itier from Tirlemenont in the Brabant and Norman from the county of Saint-Pol sur Ternoise, have an identical vision. The Virgin appears to them and asks them to warn Monseigneur Lambert, the Bishop of Arras, that on the night of Whit Sunday a woman dressed exactly like her will appear holding a wax candle in her hand. Now since the murder of Itier's brother by Norman a deadly hate has separated the two minstrels. However the Bishop allowed himself to be convinced by the tale of the two former enemies. The three men go together into the chancel of the cathedral of Notre Dame where the Virgin Mary appears as foretold holding in her hand a *"candle burning with the divine flame"*. A few drops of this wax spilled in the water brings an end to the epidemic. Everyone recovers except for a poor devil who scorns the divine remedy and dares to proclaim that he *"would rather have wine"*.... *"he becomes so engulfed in this holy flame that soon afterwards he dies, like a madman."*

This candle is still preserved at the *Musée des Beaux Arts* in the reliquary of 1215. Every year it is brought out in May for the procession of the *Ardents*. The stained glass windows of *Notre Dame-en-Cité* tell the story of the miracle. Like the squares of the town centre the *Sainte-Chandelle* continues to travel down the ages.

Jeanne's dungeon

"If you don't behave..." are there any little Arrageois who haven't trembled at the thought of being shut in the dungeon of Jeanne d'Arc? The dungeon exists...or so legend would have it. The proof? You can go down to it from the school playground of the *Collège Saint-Joseph...*

Jeanne d'Arc was held prisoner in Arras between July and November 1430 while the town was under the control of Burgundy. Philippe le Bon was still allied with the English. Jeanne, handed over in exchange for ten thousand Ecus, was transferred to Crotoy.

Four different places contest the whereabouts of Jeanne's dungeon; the *Porte Ronville,* now the site of the Post Office; the *Cour le Comte* with the dungeon of the *Collège Saint-Joseph;* the prisons of the Manor of which the dungeon was recently discovered during the renovation of the theatre; and the *Château de Bellemotte* in Saint-Laurent-Blangy - which is the favourite of the historians.

The Accursed Kings

With Jean Piat and Philippe Torreton in the costumes of Robert d'Artois, Hélène Duc and Jeanne Moreau playing Mahaut, Claude Barma and Josée Dayan have managed to make this story popular on television.

In the historical novel of Maurice Druon, Mahaut d'Artois, poisoner and conspirator, will go to any lengths to keep hold of the Artois and to dispossess her nephew Robert III.

The fact remains that she came to power thanks to the specific terms of the laws of succession of the county of Artois, which ran contrary to the principle of the male right of inheritance in force in the rest of the kingdom.

Despite being somewhat authoritarian, Mahaut is remembered by the Arrageois for her support for the arts and for communal liberty. Her account books record a wide generosity towards the monasteries and the town's hospitals.

Robert d'Artois, for his part, as a result of bitterness and a series of unsuccessful legal battles, eventually entered into alliance with Edward III, King of England. What had been a family affair was to escalate into the Hundred Years' War. One of the epilogues of this was the treaty of Arras of 21st September 1435 which sealed the reconciliation of Philippe Le Bon, Duke of Burgundy with King Charles VII of France.

Rats and Cats

The Viscount totters. Cyrano de Bergerac punctuates the duel and the ballad with the famous...

"As I end the refrain...thrust home!"... D'Artagnan steps forward, hand held out; *"Monsieur, permit me to say that you are a fine swordsman, and I am a good judge of such things. I stamp my feet to show my admiration!"* If it is a surprise that the two characters should meet in literature, the reality is even more extraordinary. Savinien de Bergerac (the real Cyrano) and Charles de Batz Castelmore d'Artagnan were both involved in the siege of Arras in 1640 following which the town was handed over finally to France.

Within the besieged town it was proclaimed *"When the French take (prendre) Arras the rats will eat the cats"*. On 9th August 1640, after 60 days of siege, the Spanish garrison surrendered. By changing just one letter in the French we are left with *"the day the French surrender (rendre) Arras the rats will eat the cats"*.

The Romance of Vidocq

"I was born in Arras. My regular dressing up, the mobility of my features and an unusual gift for disguise which leaves a certain doubt as to my age, mean that it is not unnecessary to state that I came into the world on 23rd July 1775 in a house next door to the one where Robespierre had been born 16 years earlier." Vidocq was born the son of a baker at *222 rue du Miroir-de-Venise...* now called *rue des Trois-Visages* (of the Three Faces)!

From the time of his adolescence he was nicknamed *le Vautrin*, – a wild boar in the local Artois dialect. Things took a turn for the worse when at sixteen years of age he left home, taking with him the family savings. In 1794 he married Marie-Anne-Louise Chevalier in Arras with whom he ran a grocer's shop. A brief interlude. The legend is under way. Crook, soldier, convict, notorious for his escapes from the prisons at both Brest and Toulon, he ended up as head of the *Brigade de Sûreté* in Paris (Criminal Investigations Department of Paris). Vidocq is familiar with both the dregs of society and with high society. *'Ah, Monsieur Balzac, if I had your writer's skills I would write things which would shake up the sky and earth from top to bottom...'* he writes to the author of the *Comédie Humaine*. In 1828 Vidocq publishes his *Mémoires,* together with some novels and a dictionary of slang. Common people make their first appearance in literature. It was from the Arrageois that Hugo derived the material to write *Le Dernier Jour d'un Condamné* (The Last Day of a Condemned Man)

Jean Valjean (and Javert) in *Les Misérables* are both based on Vidocq, as is Balzac's Vautrin and Eugène Sue's Rodolphe de Sombreuil, Poe's Dupin and Dumas' Jackal d'Alexandre.

Even in his literary glory his identities are multiple. At every street corner, Arras affords material for a romantic novel.

'Impasse du
Chevalier-Rouge'.

Scandal at the station

'It was Paul Verlaine's idea wasn't it? / Did you have the time to call and see his mother that morning? / Was it Verlaine who at the last minute chose the Gare du Nord rather than the Gare de l'Est? / I would like to think that your cardigan was ideal / On the platform of the station of Arras / Tell me, after your tipple with the two gendarmes? / Eh, Tizot', eun'tiote bistoule? (and you, a small gin and coffee?) / Quatre'tiotes bistoules? (four small gin and coffees?) Have you never had gin before?'

In her extended poem *Questions à Arthur Rimbaud* the Arras-based poet Sylvie Nève explores and develops a real event in the history of Arras, the scandal of the station which occurred on 8th July 1872. The night before, whilst searching for a doctor for his wife Mathilde, Verlaine bumped into Rimbaud who asked him to decide once and for all between his wife and his *liberté libre*, his full freedom. Verlaine offered no resistance to Rimbaud, *"l'homme aux semelles de vent"*, but in order to reassure himself he took his friend to his home town of Arras. Early the following morning at the station café the poets drank a little more than they should and provoked an informer on the table next to them by inventing murders and thefts they had *"committed"* and filling in with the most gruesome and vivid details. Petit, the prosecutor, realised that it was all a joke and the following day Verlaine and Rimbaud were put back on the train by the constabulary. Before leaving they negotiated a few rounds with the *Gendarmes... "Eun'tiote bistoule?"*

Verlaine, home town

Arras, starting point...point of return. When things went wrong following the Commune, the prison of Mons and the escapades with Rimbaud, Verlaine always returned to his home town. A place for repentance and relaxation.

"In my mother's country the land is fertile, and a man, gentle but strong, can live, a prince of the plain ..."

Madame Verlaine, the mother, used to keep her foetuses in preserving jars. Following four miscarriages she finally gave birth to Paul Verlaine on 30th March 1844 in Metz.

Lecluse, home of Elisa Moncomble, the cousin to whom he avows a true passion, and Fampoux, where he visits his uncle Julien Dehée are the places of his earliest emotional experiences. Verlaine especially enjoyed the route along the Scarpe which leads from Fampoux to the station of Arras; a route scattered with temptation, cafes, fairs and brothels.

In his *Confessions* he doesn't hide this from us. *"I used to drink a lot when I went to my uncle's in Fampoux near Arras, l'breune and chel'blinque and g'nief, to say nothing of the bistoules"*. Just before his marriage to Mathilde he confided to a friend that he had *"given up all the insobriety and all the phallic journeys to Arras; I want to be worthy of her!"*

Later Verlaine was to return in order to escape his personal demons. The house on the *impasse d'Elbronne* where his mother, Eliza, moved in 1875 was a haven. "Arras is dear to me for a thousand reasons; family ties, its overall calm and supreme beauty" he wrote in *Vieille Ville*. *"At the end of the aisle in the gothic church, against the wall which mystic daylight comes to kiss"* a vision appears to him in the church of Saint-Géry: *"the crucifix rises up ineffably gentle"*. It's the moment of *Sagesse.*

He sings the praises of Arras to his Parisien friends...

"So white are the old houses, so well built / Not high, here and there branches on their ridges / Such a gentle and winding shape these houses form / Like a stream among the waves of foliage / Which shape the light and shade into embroidery / Rather than the extended tedium of your haussmanneries..."

Place des Héros (Heroes Square): the 'Suspended Forest'.
Collective Lucie Lom, March 2004. ➤

26   Ruins of the Town Hall and of the Belfry photographed by Joseph Quentin.
From the collection of the Arras Museum of Fine Arts.

HISTORY REDISCOVERED

« La ville ne se livre pas de prime abord. Elle résiste. Elle se livre mais en douceur. Tous les jours, je croise des gens qui ont deux mille ans d'histoire. Marcher dans la rue est un voyage continuel dans le temps. »

Alain Jacques

The photographs by Joseph Quentin assault the imagination. The framing gives a measure of the damage sustained in the course of war. Arras is the Verdun of the North. From the very beginning of the conflict the city is a fortified camp. The slow methodical destruction of the buildings begins on 6th October 1914. Any eminence which might be used as an observation post – the belfry, the *hôtel de ville,* the church of Saint-Jean-Baptiste – is destroyed by artillery fire. On 21st October the belfry collapses. The town squares are reduced to ruins. Its inhabitants abandon the city. The cathedral is under continuous bombardment from 24th to 29th May 1915. *"The shelling, by large calibre artillery, is no longer accompanied by the high-pitched whistling that we are familiar with, but by a slow yet powerful rumbling, the death-rattle of the earth"* writes Henry Gruy in *Histoire d'Arras.* On 5th July the *Abbaye Saint-Vaast* is ablaze. For three days *"the Germans relentlessly shower the blaze with time shells and percussion shells"* The library, town archives and the museum are reduced to a pile of rubble.

Everything is real, yet everything is false. The idea of rebuilding the city exactly as it was is rooted in the traumatic experience itself. To supplement the war damages, donations towards the rebuilding of the town flood in from all around; above all from Marseille and from Newcastle-upon-Tyne which adopted the city. The plan of reconstruction is approved with a decisive vote by the *Conseil Municipal* (municipal council) on 16th March 1923. The work is entrusted to the architect Pierre Paquet. The *Hôtel de Ville,* relieved of its 2nd Empire extensions is restored to its original beauty. The interior décor matches the exterior; French Renaissance style for the main body of the building and Flemish Renaissance for the wings. The *Salle des Fêtes* on the first floor, with its paintings by Charles Hoffbauer, is like an immense comic strip in the style of Bruegel, where, always with humour, we flick backwards and forwards from the past to the present. On the town squares two thirds of the houses have been destroyed; a gigantic puzzle. Fragments of decoration are recovered from the ruins and used as moulds. With the stone from Saint Maximin the facades on the city squares recover the lustre and harmony of the centuries gone by. Pierre Paquet makes use of the latest technology in the service of history. The facades rest against a structure of reinforced concrete. The same principle is used for the belfry where the use of concrete enables the Arras engineer Louis Peulabeuf to solve the historic problem posed by the instability of the land and by the underground tunnels.

Far from being a pastiche, the reconstruction is exemplary. It captures the spirit, memory and life of the place. This is fundamental. Arras or a fairy story, *"a deception which conveys the truth"*. The archaeologist Alain Jacques expresses this in his unique style *"the town doesn't give itself away at first glance. It resists, opening up little by little. Each day I meet people who have two thousand years of history. Walking in the street is a continual voyage through time."*

The mind wanders. Between the *Maison des Trois Luppars,* already rebuilt in 1467, and the town which dates almost entirely from the Enlightenment, lies a collection of startling contrasts. The Mont-de-Piété rises above the roof tops. The *Place Victor Hugo* surprises with its octagonal form, designed by Pierre-Louis Beffara who drew his inspiration from the *Hôtel de Beaufort,* built in 1754 in a neighbouring street. The square was originally home to the livestock market; the sandstone blocks with their rings still survive.

In the heart of the town the eighteenth century *hôtels particuliers* close in around their ostentatious front courtyards. Within Arras' own "small Paris Saint-Germain" the passions and ambition are in proportion to the setting. To the right is Alexandre Gonsse de Rougeville, also known as the "Knight of the *Maison Rouge*", born in Arras in 1761. In 1793 he attempted to rescue Louis XVI from his executioners. In love with the Queen, he also tried to free Marie-Antionette from the *Conciergerie* by slipping a message into a bouquet of carnations.

Involved in the assination attempt against Bonaparte in 1800, and in the *Complot de Cadoudal* in 1804, the tireless conspirator remained faithful to his monarchist beliefs until he died on 10th March 1814, executed by firing squad on the *Champ de Mars.*

To the left is Maximilien Robespierre, the young lawyer who became integrated into the high society of Arras. On 4th February 1786 he was appointed director of the Academy of Arras and was introduced into the circle of Lazare Carnot. The same year the future mayor, Dubois de Fosseux makes him member of the Rosati Poets' Society where he welcomes him with a few verses in... patois.

Pour sin confrere tout nouviau (for our new fellow member)
Chest un garchon qu'ia du cerveau (he is a very clever boy)
Pour l'intind' quand i divise (to hear him when he talks)
Eh bien! (Well!)
J'barrouais l'mitant de m'qu'mise (I would give half of my shirt)

Champion of the poor and author of a tract on *"the rights and conditions of illegitimate children",* he enjoys a certain popularity and draws up a register of grievances for the cobblers of Arras. Dubois de Fosseux becomes a political opponent. Maximilien hurls the name of a family of common birth at him saying *"one day the Lantillettes will govern this town."* The revolution has started. It shows no mercy. In a guide written in 1913 the Abbot Raymond Drimille, teacher at Saint-Joseph, lets loose evoking the *"evil Robespierre"* and the *"blood-thirsty Joseph Lebon"* who was present on the balcony of the theatre at the *"torture of his fellow citizens, whom he had sent to the guillotine."* His observations are gruesome: *"What tragedy this floor would tell us if only it were possible for it to cry out the names of those whose blood it has tasted!"*

The people of Arras would long harbour a feeling of betrayal towards Robespierre. The relationship between *'L'Incorruptible'* Robespierre and his native town has not been straightforward. On 15th October 1933 the planned inauguration of a statue came to an abrupt halt. The town awoke to find two wooden guillotines set up on the town's squares, dummies dressed as aristocrats hanging from the lamposts, cardboard heads swinging and red paint running in the gutters. In 1968 the *Comité d'action lycéenne* fought to name their school after Robespierre... however, the establishment has never been officially inaugurated.

The Pawnshop, 1624, located in the rue du Marché-au-Filé. ➤

The situation seems nowadays to have cooled. *"Our perception of history is more discriminating,"* explains Christian Lescureux, Secretary of the Association Les *Amis de Robespierre.* *"We mustn't forget that the 'Incorruptible' Robespierre held, above all else, a passion for equality...without which he believed liberty to be just an empty word. He is the key character in the Revolution, the saviour of the Republic and the inventor of universal suffrage. He is a person of considerable importance, and known throughout the world. He deserves better than his caricature."*

Between Robespierre and Arras there's still not much love lost, but attitudes are changing. Opposite the theatre a street is named after him. The house where he lived between 1787 and 1789 has been restored and has become a museum of the *Compagnons du Tour de France.* In 2001 the *musée des Beaux Arts* acquired a portrait of this child of their land.

With its elegance and sophistication, and *hôtels particuliers,* Arras remains very much a town of the eighteenth century. A town of the Enlightenment which despite its political and industrial revolutions retains an aristocratic flavour. No real break with the past, just history which is forever renewing and recycling itself.

When the revolution breaks out work on the new St Vaast Abbey-Church, entrusted to the Parisian architect Constant d'Ivry, is almost complete. The monks are chased out and their belongings confiscated. On his visit to Arras on 29th August 1804 Napoleon decides to complete work on the Abbey-Church St Vaast but gives orders for the destruction of the ancient cathedral Notre-Dame-en-Cité on the *Colline Baudimont,* which is too badly damaged.

◄ Saint-Vaast Abbey. 18th Century Italian-style drawing room. Entrance hall of the Museum of Fine Arts.

Devastated by an incendiary bomb on 6th July 1915, the new cathedral has to be rebuilt. With its majestic lines the building has something of the *Panthéon*. The nave is enormous. Eight huge statues of saints keep watch in the ambulatory. These statues originate from the church of Sainte-Geneviève in Paris before it became the *Temple des Grands Hommes*. Construction, destruction, reconstruction, renovation, excavation, discovery; history is being eternally created.

On 1st February 2003 the curtain falls on the theatre. It rises again on 15th February 2007. Meanwhile, renovation work uncovers remains of the medieval tower of the donjon. These had been incorporated into the ancient *Salle des Orphéonistes*. It was known that the theatre à l'Italienne, opened on 30th November 1785 had been built on the site of the old municipal prisons in the ancient fortified buildings belonging to the first *Chatelain* of Arras. *"The carbon 14 identification shows that the remains of the donjon underneath the theatre date back to the eleventh century"* declares Alain Jacques.

New discoveries sometimes call received knowledge into question. The town archaeologist doesn't tire of this *"the wonder never ceases. It was always believed that the theatre square was the oldest square, but now the excavations have shown us not a square but remains of the outbuildings of the residence of the seigneur; the chapel, the kitchens…"*. The story of the town has yet to be written. The charm is at work, and has been for over two thousand years.

Archaeological excavation of the hall of the theatre. ➤

TODAY, TOMORROW

« Arras est un mille-feuille d'histoires. »

Jean-Marie Prestaux

"Since the loss of the earthly paradise we no longer possess eternity...Hence the need to measure time". In the Seneca family the trade of clockmaker has passed from father to son since 1720. They have been established in Arras since 1836.
Chancellor of the Academy of Arts, founded in 1737, and faithful to the Rosati Society just like his grandfather Raoul who "entertained painters and poets", Bernard Seneca, President of the Office Culturel created in 2000, likes to speak of "emotions" and of "inter-personal skills." Named best craftsman of France, the clockmaker and restorer follows on in the demanding tradition of the master craftsman. One reason he takes apart and reassembles mechanisms from the past is in order to be able better to scan the present and make projections for the future: "From the theatre with André Reybaz to the Centre Noroit for contemporary Art, Arras has always enjoyed a very rich cultural life. It is still the case today with the Quai de la Batterie which has taken over in the field of plastic arts, with the Salon du Livre d'Expression Populaire (a book fair aimed at the general public), with contemporary song and the association Di Dou Da, with Plan Séquence and the International Film Festival."
It is evidence of this vitality that the Office Culturel brings together over eighty different associations. "The aim is to give each association the means to develop, and to enable people to meet and work together." From the village which is set up for the festival L'Autre Cinéma on Grand'Place in November to the more traditional festivals and fairs, from the traditional Northern harmonies to the trendy concerts and nights of jazz, the people of Arras are nourished with a regular variation between tradition and modernity.
This movement is written in stone. Immediately after the Great War the reconstruction was driven by two differing philosophies; on the one hand a desire to preserve the wealth of the past, and on the other the need to invent a future. New main roads were driven through, new shopping areas were opened... Architects vied with one another in their creativity; Art Deco facades on the rue Saint-Aubert, houses around the place de la Vacquerie built in the traditional regional style, modern red brick "crow-stepped gables" on the rue Delansorne. The urban landscape reflects the diversity of a town which is going places.
Each opportunity, such as the buildings in the town centre recently vacated by the religious community of the Ursulines, opens new possibilities for development.
The Mayor, Jean-Marie Vanlerenberghe cites the network of paths, the "trame verte" which runs along the Crinchon and the "trame bleue" which runs along the Scarpe. In the historic centre the plan is to draw up a trail which will lead from the Jardin Minelle to the Citadelle Vauban, passing through the woods of the Prefecture.

◄ Clock components, Empire style.

At the North entrance to the town a watersports centre will open in 2011, just alongside the *Cité Nature*. A large area of walks is planned along the valley of the Scarpe between Arras Golf Course and the *Guinguette* (open air café) in Fampoux. A lake for competitive rowing and paddling should shortly be completed on the site of the old river port, beside the existing spring water lake at Laurent-Blangy. For the London Olympics of 2012 Arras will be the training base for the canoe and kayak teams.

After the Belfry, the *Citadelle Vauban* – the famous *"Useless Beauty"*- was officially recognised in 2008 as a UNESCO World Heritage Site. There are few towns in the world which can boast two buildings in this prestigious list! The theatre of Arras, fully renovated in its Italian setting, is enjoying a new lease of life, and the Wellington Quarries are now open to the public. People come from all over the world to immerse themselves once more in the emotion of the 1917 Battle of Arras.

The town's squares remain unshakeable, as beautiful as a dream of stone... but so alive. The *Place des Héros* on a market day, where you can rediscover the fragrance of the countryside, is vividly captured by the writer Paul Adam in 1919... *"the bread from Héricourt Mill, the peas from Saint-Laurent, the freshly fried fish from the Scarpe, the chicken from Souchez, roasted and ready to eat; the pigeons from Vimy skilfully prepared in fricasse, the beef from Beaurains, vegetables from Achicourt, beer from Saint-Nicolas, cherries from Blangy, redcurrants from Mercatel."*

Grand'Place, amazing in summer with *Arras on the Beach* where volleyball, baseball and rugby can all be played on the sand.

Grand'Place where the historian Alain Nolibos feels at home, at the heart of Europe. *"We are at the point of the crescent which links*

◄ Variety of Art Déco styles, rue Paul Doumer.

the Northern Baroque towns. From Arras to Saint Petersburg passing through Ghent, Bremen, Kraków and Tallinn, the same spirit breathes."

Simone de Beauvoir confides: *"within two hours from Paris the only urban landscape which has truly enraptured me is the assemblage of the large and small town squares of Arras"*

Grand'Place on a quiet morning: *"One day I think I'm bound to tire of it, but each time I am surprised by some new detail or a certain new light,"* admits Nelly Dupré one of the town guides.

"Arras is a mille-feuille, a thousand layers of history", the expression is from Jean-Marie Prestaux, the Director of the Tourist Office.

Grand'Place on the days when there are festivals and special concerts. The *Main Square Festival* is the only festival in Europe to be staged in the centre of a town of forty five thousand inhabitants. The hundred thousand people who squeeze in each year to see Depeche Mode, Metallica or Céline Dion are simply the heirs and descendants of those who took part in the *Fête de la Fédération,* organised by Dubois de Fosseux, and held in the same place, on 3rd June 1790.

The clocks which chime, the speeches and the music, the parades by the troops and the *Garde Nationaux... Grand'Place* throughout the ages has been the setting for changes of regime, royal visits and religious or secular festivals.

On 14th July 1790 the idea of Dubois de Fosseux was taken up in Paris on the *Champs-de-Mars;* this is the origin of the National Festival.

Arras, town of history, constantly opens up new routes to the future.

'Depeche Mode' playing in the Main Square, June 2006. ➤

THE PASSION OF THE ARTIST

« Détresse – en qui je puise la matière / de mon poème –, enseigne-moi /
ce dérivatif : y exposer mon triste état »…
« Détresse, toi qui inondes mon cœur, / Salue pour moi Arras »…

Jean Bodel

Jean Bodel of Arras
TROUBADOUR AND PLAYWRIGHT

Jean Bodel, first floor
landing. Town Hall

The theatre was born in Arras. For more than twenty years, Sylvie Nève has been fascinated by the literary effervescence which set the town ablaze between 1180 and 1280. *"The modernity of the troubadours wouldn't exist if it hadn't been for the wealth around at that moment in time."* Picture it: the King of France owes thousands of pounds to the usurers in Arras. King Henry III of England pawns his silver with a certain Bertoul Verdière. The silver gets passed around. Merchants and bankers are dabbling at poetry, and sponsoring the arts, sometimes even paying ghostwriters. The *'je'* enters into literature. Arras becomes the town of eighty poets. Among them is Jean Bodel, inventor of the modern theatre.

Le Jeu de Saint Nicolas is first performed on 5th December 1200. Bodel introduces a secular space – a tavern – on to the stage, which allows him to evoke the life of his contemporaries. In 1276, Adam de la Halle goes even further with Le Jeu de la Feuillée, a kind of comic opera which examines the faults of society. *"I have always dreamt of Arras opening a theatre museum because this is where it all started,"* says Sylvie Nève.

In 1202, Bodel, suffering from leprosy, takes his leave from the world of the living with *Les Congés* (Leave Takings). At the moment of his departure, he invents a new form of writing. *"In trouvère (troubador) there is trouveur (finder)"* explains Sylvie Nève. *Les Congés* is a wonderful portrayal of human dignity when faced with a disease which is eating him away.

'Distress - from which I draw the substance / of my poem – grant me / this relief: to reveal therein my sad condition' / 'Distress, as you overwhelm my heart / Say farewell to Arras on my behalf ...'

From Rutebeuf to Villon – through to Jacques Brel – Jean Bodel marks the beginning of one of the major themes in modern poetry.

"Adieu l'Émile je t'aimais bien ..." (Goodbye to you, my trusted friend...)

Sylvie Facon

FASHION DESIGNER AND VISUAL ARTIST

« Je travaille sur des coups de cœur. Je suis sensible aux seins,
aux hanches. J'aime les femmes. Une robe, c'est un regard
sensible sur la beauté d'un être. »

"A star so close and yet so far away…" The poems of her friend José Ambre suit Sylvie Facon perfectly, in all her brilliance. Julie and Léa, fashion models in today's world; Lucie who discovers herself a woman on the morning the world began: the entire creative output of this *Arrageoise* designer is a hymn to beauty. *"I work on impulse, on coups de coeur. I am particularly aware of the breasts and the hips. I like women. A dress is a sensitive presentation of the beauty of a person.'* The dresses she has created include one in the form of a painting – a tribute to Gustave Klimt – a Poem in Textiles, a Song of Songs, a Dream in Silk, a Water Garden, an October Whirlwind… each dress is unique, wedded to one body, one soul.

Along with dreams and fairytales, Sylvie Facon keeps her secrets hidden below the dormers of a house in Roclincourt where she renews her acquaintance with *Donkeyskin.* Dresses in the colours of the Sky, the Moon, and the Sun really exist. A princess, with a touch of the alchemist, Sylvie has penetrated the Mysteries. A self-taught visual artist, she walks a tight rope. Always patient, she even goes as far as to work on a spider web. Never once does she fall into the trap of sentimentality.

The Boldness is in the matching of the lace with the fabric of the bed, the metal with the silk, the bark with the fibre. Arras museum, the *Cité Nature,* the *Abbaye de Vaucelles,* the museum of lace at Caudry and the Jacquard museum in Roubaix all welcome dresses by Sylvie Facon in their collections. A basket of irises, a field of poppies, suddenly springing from a bodice, or from a petticoat, in a tangle of pearls and seaweed.

Behind the grace and sense of purity, the creations of the little dancer from the *corps de ballet* of Arras remain emotionally charged. Bare-handed, she has taken on the struggle against the passage of time. Like someone too full of love, she moves among the materials; as a creator, she lays herself bare. *'In Love, the anguish is diminished'* she says.

And Sylvie Facon is eternally in love.

Luc Brévart

VISUAL ARTIST, THEATRE DIRECTOR

« À huit ans, je me souviens d'un Atlas offert par mon père.
D'un côté, on découvrait Arras. De l'autre, Oulan-Bator
et la Mongolie. »

Bread. Son of a baker-confectioner established just a few yards from the belfry, Luc Brévart kneads history. Each spring, he is in charge of the festival *Allées en fêtes* held in the *Jardin du Gouverneur.* Working between fiction and reality, the director is unceasingly modelling the town, interpreting its myths and legends, such as Cyrano, Mahaut d'Artois and d'Artagnan.

Stone. The Association *Quai de la Batterie* now has its home at the *Hôtel de Guînes.* There are workshops on contemporary art, artists in residence, book fairs: Luc Brévart is a one-man band, a *missi dominici* who loves to spread the message. It is largely thanks to him that people such as the sculptor Ousmane Sow and the visual artist Wang Qing Song have been able to make such an impression on the citizens of Arras.

The sky. The glass house which Luke Brévart is building with his own hands, on the slopes of *Mont-Saint-Eloi* is a genuine work of art.

A life project. Between two stone walls engraved by the *poilus* (soldiers of the First World War) in 1914, wooden boxes stacked beneath the huge glass roof make up the living space. A Canadian well regulates the temperature. The voice of the artist, full of gentleness, is in its element here. He confides: *"At the age of eight, I remember the atlas that my father gave me. On one side, you had Arras and on the other Ulan Bator and Mongolia."* As part of a never-ending dialogue between the interior and the exterior, the bell-tower of Écoivres, clouds and a flock of migrating birds - all seem to stream past in the distance. Though a great traveller, Luc Brévart loves to return to the land of Artois. From here he draws the energy for his artwork: parchment books, cards, solar system boxes, terrestrial globes each with their open wounds. Brévart works at the open fault, the place where it hurts. Without violence but with strength.

This work forms part of an underground cosmogony where our insane desire for happiness gets mired in the mud of conflict.

The shaved head of the artist is itself a world map. This globe is an invitation. For us all to share our humanity.

Globe series II, 'war', mixed media, 2000 (detail).

Mireille Desideri

PAINTER, SCULPTOR

« Peindre, c'est éviter, passer à côté. Dans mon travail, la forme se marque par son manque. Elle s'abstient. Le pinceau ne la dessine pas, il est ailleurs, dans la surimposition des couleurs. La forme naît de son oubli. »

The display window is a beacon in the night. At *46 rue Baudimont*, the blind opens up on the possibility of discovery. In the front of her workshop and living space, she has installed *MDV*, a gallery which is to be seen but which cannot be entered. The art is on the street. Behind an enormous generosity and pleasure in sharing, hides Mireille Desideri. As the workshop door is pushed open the light streams out. The old Lada garage is now a huge laboratory of shapes. Mireille Desideri is reluctant to say too much about her work. The workshop is a hollow space. A place for painting, where anything might be created. She writes: *"Painting is avoiding, going round things. In my work, the shape is noticeable by its absence. The shape is withheld. The brush doesn't draw it; it is elsewhere, within the superimposition of the colours. The shape emerges from its omission."*

Flint is at the heart of her work. Since 1990, she has been bringing them back from the marlpits of Artois and storing them in her workshop. A task of accumulation reminiscent of the quest for Art Brut. *"But I'm too exacting..."* The battle with the shapes is the same. *"This particular fight is a just one".* There is something of the essence of what it is to be human in the gesture of Mireille Desideri. Beauty – bones, genitals, woman, bird – springs from chance, out of nothing. In her collaboration with Sylvie Nève on *Érotismées,* the blank space and the impossible are comparable to the emotion and the inexpressible. The drawing is an integral part of the words of the writer:

'Par dessous m'aborde / déborde-moi le noir / s'y boire d'il le cri / Dedans.'

Gentleness and violence. Suspended moments. Time is at work. The hard water of Arras drops its sediment in the hollow of the sculpture *Les Gisants.* It calls to mind the reclining effigy of Guillaume Lefranchois, a superb exhibit in the *Musée des Beaux-Arts d'Arras. 'Clarity of the visible is only possible through awareness of the empty space'.* The workshop of Mireille Desideri is built on the forum of the ancient city of Nemetacum

'Gisants', epoxy, 2002.

Sylvie Nève

POET, MEDIAEVALIST, PSYCHOANALYST

« Il était une fois, poils, cailloux / bijoux, fée, foi d'animal /
roi et reine, aux temps chauds / ne songeant pas / au malheur. »

Sylvie Nève tells things as they are. She has made herself a list of one hundred and seventeen abusive terms for a writer... "Witch – Sucker – Poet – Female – Formalist - (....)" "I don't like to sweetenen things up" she warns, from the kitchen of her home in *Rue de la Caisse d'Epargne*. "At the turn of the century society ladies would come here to have their portraits taken by the photographer Mademoiselle Chrétien. Across the road there was a brothel for the gentlemen". She has a passion for unearthing the seamy side of things.

Daughter of the mineral workings, of the *"voyettes"* (small paths) and slag heaps around Carvin, Sylvie Nève has lived and worked in Arras for more than twenty five years. As a mediaevalist she is at home between Jean Bodel, Baude Fastol and Adam de la Halle. As a writer who likes to experiment in new forms she is equally at home.

In 1200 Bodel writes *Le Jeu de Saint Nicolas,* the first ever miracle play in common language. At the end of the twentieth century Sylvie Nève writes a minimal light opera *Poèmeshow* together with Jean-Pierre Bobillot. In 1202 Jean Bodel, fallen victim to leprosy, isn't satisfied with the promise of eternal life. Between 1st July 1988 and 30th June 1989 Sylvie Nève interviews people each Friday and then publishes *De Partout.* A modern Antigone, scratching at the truth turning over the words... She demonstrates a real pleasure in sharing - in her many artistic collaborations, in her practice of psychoanalysis, and in enjoying a shared *tarte au libouli* (boiled milk flan).

Today, in her extended poem Sylvie Nève revisits *Peau d'Ane* (Donkey Skin)...

"Once upon a time, hair, stones / jewels, fairy, animal's word, King and Queen, in the warm months / unable to imagine / misfortune".

She writes about Gaza, which *"has become an uproar in the world"*, and takes Rimbaud by the hand. *"Would you like to come back to Arras? By train, like the first time? But alone? Do you think you will stay for a few days? But then, tell me, shall we still go to Aden?"*

Once upon a time there was... Sylvie Nève, a great lady of poetry.

Catherine Slowik

PAINTER

« Mes racines sont polonaises et russes. Ma grand-mère est Ukrainienne. Je suis retournée à Charna, dans son village. J'ai découvert que "Charna" veut dire "noir". »

Her godmother, Huguette Verwaerde, was the caretaker... *"My first square would have been the curtain of the theatre of Arras."* Catherine Slowik delves into her past; she recalls the darkroom of her parents, both photographers, settled for years at 23 *place des Héros.* She also pictures *"the frontages of the town squares"* and the memory of her uncle Michel. *"I must have been seven years old. I asked him to draw me a square with a wooden ruler. I was absolutely fascinated."*

The meeting with Catherine Slowik is face to face. The painting is raw. *"I've got the Slavic temperament which modulates from major to minor, from chaos to melancholy."* Looking for starting points. *"My roots are both Polish and Russian. My grandmother is Ukrainian. I returned to her village in Charna where I discovered that 'Charna' means 'black'."*

The physical components of the frame are in place, but the whole adventure of painting cannot come to life without a deep questioning of the world around. She quotes Malevitch: *"Darkness has risen and the sun, coated with a layer of culture, has died ..."*

Catherine Slowik fights with bare hands. She is working on *The Bride's Veil,* and has driven twenty thousand pins into the fabric. On one side a field of mother-of-pearl, on the other metal points. The duality is a regular feature of her work. She paints in the darkness, from which forms arise by chance, coming out of the night. She explores the square which gives structure to the space, in which talismans, fragments and secrets slip into view, partially obscured by the darkness of the material. *"I am the only one to know."* A life stable, but liable to explode.

In her home in Acheville an angel keeps watch. It was given to her by the painter Stani Nitkowski, a friend from the days of wild laughter, who committed suicide in 2001. The boundaries seem to lack meaning. Green activist, teacher, researcher at the Sorbonne, artist, Catherine Slowik is a woman of conviction. An explosive cocktail of impetuosity and extreme rigour. *"I'm a woman of passion"* she says. In Polish, *slowick* means *rossignol...* the nightingale

Jacques Leclercq-K

TEACHER, PAINTER, LAND ARTIST

« Elle a semé du lin vivace / dans le Brabant pour toujours /
et maintenant / il y a un papillon qui se pose /
sur les fragments du temps. »

Henri Falaise

The eye is insatiable. Man loves to communicate. Jacques Leclercq-K teaches still-life and real-life drawing at *l'Ecole Supérieure des métiers d'Arts*. *"With my friend Yves Faure, the director, I relive what I enjoyed as a student. The school has a long tradition in stained glass, ceramics, sculpture and set design while being open to other disciplines. It combines rigour and generosity with innovation."* Jacques Leclercq-K is a man who likes to sow seeds. The countryman and the artist, both have a similar notion of time, and of the moment frozen in time. *"She has sown hardy flax / in the Brabant for all time / and now / there is a butterfly which settles on the fragments of time,"* writes the Belgian poet Henri Falaise.

Jacques Leclercq-K has planted blue oilseed flax in Picardy in the Friolet valley, a dry valley abandoned by water several million years ago. Its suspended river stretches out over four kilometres. For the artist of the land, it all starts as a daydream. This is followed by the sketch-book, the outline drawing, the nourishment drawn from both written texts and meetings. Then follows the team work; with the providers of the seeds, Labouret Semences, and the farmers. *"I like to slip into the production process."* You have to be alone ... but at the same time supported on all sides. To be convincing. Able to take others with you into the adventure. Once out on the ground, the drawing is done by the tractor. Getting the colour wash to work when the earth dries out, when the rain makes itself scarce. *"In solidarity, almost by capillary action, I finished up feeling what it must be to be a plant,"* writes Jacques Leclercq-K in his log. Then the moment of grace. Rain. The blue wash is no longer just on the studio walls. It is here, like cut paper in the middle of the countryside. A plainsong. The variation of shades with the breakthrough here and there of red poppies, california poppies and red flax. Then the colour which meanders, the redness of the flax once the flower has withered, the whirring of the bees and the rustling of the dried flax; the starlings and land gulls. The creative gesture is itself creator. A tender but hungry eye focussed on the world.

'River of flax', 2006

Christian Carion

FILM DIRECTOR

« Lors des labours, je ramassais des schrapnels, les éclats d'obus allemands, et des fusils rouillés. Mon grand-père me racontait la Grande Guerre. »

Arras, city of cinema. From 1970, the town squares were used by Costa Gravas to depict Prague in his film *L'Aveu. La Glaneuse* by Jules Breton, located in the *Musée des Beaux Arts,* is the starting point of Agnès Varda's film *Les Glaneurs et La Glaneuse.*

Since 2000, the film festival *Plan-Séquence* has welcomed directors as prestigious as Francesco Rosi, Volker Schlöndorff, Bertrand Tavernier, Sydney Lumet, Claude Chabrol and Arthur Penn. *"The spirit of the international festival which is held in November, is Auteur Cinéma for the general public",* stresses Nadia Paschetto who is responsible for the festival. *"The emphasis is on conviviality. Directors like Chabrol fall under the spell of the city, break away from us and flee into the streets. The idea is to provide young people with the chance to see the films which trace the history of cinema, and to discover how these classics still have an influence on contemporary film-making. The* Leçon de Cinéma, *organised in conjunction with the* Université d'Artois, *aims at doing just that."*

Christian Carion, nominated for an Oscar in 2006, is in the tradition of film makers who can move people at the deepest emotional level. Born on 4th of January 1963 in Cambrai to farming parents, he grew up in Lebucquière, close to Bapaume, twenty-seven kilometres from Arras. *"Just like everyone else, during the ploughing, I would collect shrapnel, fragments of German shells, and old rusty rifles. My grandfather used to tell me about the Great War. Above all else, I remember the British cemeteries and all the soldiers who were buried just where they fell."*

Christian Carion remembers *"the celebrations of the 15th August and discovering the films shown at the* centre Noroit." *"Later on",* he confides, *"I worked for five years at the Direction Départementale d'Agriculture. Arras was a good time of my life."*

Joyeux Noël was shot in Barlin and at the *Château de Brias* near Saint-Pol-sur-Ternoise. Christian Carion had been carrying the story with him since 1993 and his discovery of the book *Battles of Flanders and Artois 1914-1918* by Yves Buttefaut. Everything is true ... The fraternizing in the trenches, the midnight mass, the tenor, the christmas trees. The land still carries the memory of these events: *"An important part of European history was played out in Artois."*

Pine sanctuary in Vimy, dedicated to the
canadian solders.

BIBLIOGRAPHY

Arras, de Nemetacum à la Communauté urbaine. Alain Nolibos. Éditions La Voix du Nord.
Pignons sur rues. Jean-Marie Prestaux. Philippe Druon. Office de tourisme d'Arras.
Les places d'Arras. Martine Proy, Itinéraires du patrimoine.
Histoire d'Arras sous la direction de Pierre Bougard, Yves-Marie Hilaire et Alain Nolibos. Éditions Le Téméraire.
Histoire d'Arras. Henry Gruy. Éditions culture et civilisation.
Arras et l'Arrageois. Régis Bernet. Punch Éditions.
Méaulens - Saint-Géry. Ouvrage collectif. Éditions Alan Sutton.
Arras ville antique. Alain Jacques. Service archéologique Arras, 2000.
Les beffrois. Pierre Henry, Éditions La Voix du Nord.
Les donjons de la liberté. Catherine Dhérent et Jean-Luc A. d'Asciano. Éditions du Quesne.
La cathédrale d'Arras. Plaquette Office de tourisme.
La Grande Reconstruction. Archives départementales du Pas-de-Calais, 2002.
Le musée des Beaux-Arts. Annick Notter et Guillaume Ambroise, Réunion des musées nationaux.
Histoire d'un miracle. La sainte Chandelle d'Arras. Hélène Portiglia. Musée des Beaux-Arts d'Arras.
Le musée apprivoisé. Édition Muses, Musons, Musée.
Vidocq. Études réunies par Sylvie Thorel-Cailleteau. Revue Nord'.
Sur les pas des écrivains. Balade en Pas-de-Calais. Éditions Alexandrines.
Verlaine. Histoire d'un corps. Alain Buisine. Tallandier.
Corot. Dominique Horbez. La Renaissance du Livre.
Les Congés de Jean Bodel. Entremis de l'ancien français par Sylvie Nève et Jean-Pierre Bobillot.
Centre régional de la photographie.
Érotismées. Sylvie Nève, dessins Mireille Desideri. Atelier de l'agneau.
Poèmeshow. Sylvie Nève, Jean-Pierre Bobillot. Les contemporains favoris.
Mireille Desideri. Musée des Beaux-Arts d'Arras octobre 2002 – janvier 2003.
La rivière de lin et autres fictions. Jacques Leclercq-K. Marval.

PHOTO CREDITS

© Jean-Pierre Duplan : cover and pages 4, 6, 7, 8, 9, 10, 13, 14-15, 17, 29, 25, 29, 30, 34, 35.
© Éric Le Brun : pages 2, 18, 20, 21, 31, 32, 36, 37, 38, 39, 40, 41, 42, 43, 44, 45, 46, 47, 49, 50, 51, 53.
© Joseph Quentin : page 26.
© Bernard Teissèdre : page 48, River of flax

Design: Nadia Anémiche, Lille

Translation: Gillian Kennedy and Cyrille Divry and special thanks also to Bob Kennedy for his encouragement and support.

Printed on Satimat Green paper - Vegetable based inks
Printed and bound in Spain by Artes Graficas Palermo - ISO 14001 - FSC
Registration of copyright: May 2009
ISBN : 978-2-9524717-7-0
ISSN : 1778-3038
© Light Motiv - Collection Passages en ville [éco-version]
39, rue du Pré Catelan - 59110 LA MADELEINE - http://www.lightmotiv.com - Tel. (33) 3 20 06 90 98